CITY OF FESTIVALS

Edmonton

JANICE PARKER

Published by Weigl Educational Publishers Limited
6325 – 10 Street SE
Calgary, Alberta, Canada
T2H 2Z9
Web site: http://www.weigl.com

National Library of Canada Cataloguing in Publication Data
Parker, Janice.
 Edmonton

 (Canadian Cities)
 Includes Index
 ISBN 1-896990-71-1

 1. Edmonton (Alta)--Juvenile literature. I. Title. II. Series:
Canadian Cities (Calgary, Alta)
FC3696.33.P37 2001   j971.23'34   C2001-910654-8
F1079.5.E3P37 2001

Printed and bound in Canada
1 2 3 4 5 6 7 8 9 0   05 04 03 02 01

Project Coordinator
Jill Foran
Design
Warren Clark
Cover Design
Terry Paulhus
Layout
Lucinda Cage
Photo Research
Tina Schwartzenberger

We acknowledge the
financial support of
the Government of
Canada through the
Book Publishing
Industry Development
Program (BPIDP) for
our publishing activities.

Photograph Credits
Every reasonable effort has been made to trace ownership and to obtain permission to reprint copyright material.
The publishers would be pleased to have any errors or omissions brought to their attention so that they may be
corrected in subsequent printings.

Cover: Merle Prosofsky; Inside Cover: Steve Wong; Archive Photos: page 29B; City of Edmonton Archives: page 9T
(EA-10-1386); Mike Copeman/Northlands Park: pages 3B, 21B; David Cooper/Citadel Theatre: pages 3TL, 12L;
Eyewire: page 17B; Glenbow Archives, Calgary, Canada: pages 6T (NA-1315-16), 6B (NA-1408-6), 7M (NC-6-928), 7B
(NC-6-1103), 8M (NA-1171-6), 8B (NA-614-12), 9B (NC-6-1284); Hockey Hall of Fame: pages 11T, 11R, 30B;
Legislative Assembly of Alberta: page 26; Dale MacMillan: page 21T; National Archives of Canada: page 10B
(C89581); PhotoDisc: pages 17T, 18M; Merle Prosofsky: pages 5T, 28, 29T; Provincial Museum of Alberta: pages
24MR, 24BL; Silver Fox Images: pages 5M, 12R, 13L, 13R, 15B, 16T, 23TR, 25M, 30T; John Sutton: pages 4BR,
20B, 22T, 22B; Ukrainian Archives & Museum of Alberta: page 15MR; University of Alberta: page 19L; University of
Alberta Archives: page 10T (69-112-1); D. MacMillan/Bruce Bennett Studios: page 21M; Steve Wong: pages 3TR,
5BR, 14, 16B, 18T, 18B, 19R, 20T 23TL, 23B, 25TR, 25B, 27T, 27B, 30BR.

Contents

Introduction 4

Getting There 4

Climate 4

Area and Population 5

City of Festivals 5

Interesting Statistics 5

The Past 6

Early Settlement 6

The Government 7

Law and Order 8

Early Transportation 9

Famous People . . . 10

Alexander Rutherford . . 10

Emily Murphy 10

Mark Messier 11

Wayne Gretzky 11

Culture 12

The Arts 12

Annual Celebrations . . . 13

Ethnic Cuisine 14

The Edmonton Mosaic . . 15

The Economy 16

Diverse Industries 16

Serving the City 17

Getting Around
in Edmonton 18

Smart City 19

**Sports and
Recreation** 20

Green Space 20

City of Champions 21

Tourism 22

A Trip to the Past 22

A Shopper's Delight . . . 23

Alberta's Museum 24

Muttart Conservatory . . 25

Architecture 26

A Home for the Provincial
Government 26

Restoring Older
Structures 27

Fascinating Facts . . 28

Activities 30

More Information . . 31

Glossary 32

Index 32

Introduction

Edmonton is the provincial capital of Alberta. It sits in the middle of the province, next to the North Saskatchewan River. Edmonton is known for its beautiful river valley, its festivals, and its mix of cultures.

Canada

0   500 km

Getting There

Getting to Edmonton is easy. The International Airport has flights to and from locations around the world. The Greyhound Bus Line provides transportation into Edmonton from all over North America, and Via Rail provides train service into the city. Two major highways go through Edmonton—the Yellowhead Highway and Highway 2.

At a Glance

Climate

Bright sunshine and low humidity make Edmonton's climate generally pleasant throughout all four seasons. Summer is hot and sunny, with an average high temperature of 23° Celsius. Fall can vary from warm to cool. The average high temperature in the fall months is 11°C. Edmonton usually receives its first snowfall towards the end of October. During winter, Edmonton gets plenty of snow, and its average high temperature is −11°C. Spring remains cool until April or May, with an average high of 10°C.

Area & Population

The city of Edmonton encompasses about 670 square kilometres. The Greater Edmonton Region is much larger. It includes 9,357 sq km and thirty-six municipalities. The Greater Edmonton Region has 862,597 residents, while the city itself has a population of around 658,000.

City of Festivals

Edmonton is known as the "City of Festivals" because of the many annual celebrations held in the area. The Edmonton Fringe Festival is a showcase of alternative theatre featuring a variety of plays for adults and children, as well as a food fair, buskers, and street vendors. **Klondike** Days and Heritage Days celebrate the history of the region. Other festivals celebrated in the city include the Folk Music Festival, the International Children's Festival, and Cariwest: Edmonton Caribbean Arts Festival.

Interesting Statistics

1. Edmonton has a lower population density than most other major North American cities. The population density of Edmonton is sixty-seven times lower than the population density of New York City.

2. Edmonton has more parkland per capita than any other city in Canada.

3. The Edmonton Metropolitan Region is slightly larger in area than the country of Cyprus.

4. Edmonton is the fifth largest metropolitan area in Canada, after Toronto, Montreal, Vancouver, and Ottawa-Hull.

5. Edmonton is 668 metres above sea level.

The Past

Fort Edmonton was rebuilt five times before it was moved to its permanent spot in 1930.

Early Settlement

For thousands of years, the Edmonton region was inhabited by Native Peoples who were lured by the abundance of bison and other wildlife in the area. By the eighteenth century, the Cree nation was the largest group living in the area. Many Cree had moved into the central Alberta region in order to trap animals for the European fur trade.

In 1795, the North West Company, a fur-trading company from Montreal, established Fort Augustus about 32 km from present-day Edmonton. That same year, another fur-trading company, called the Hudson's Bay Company, established a fort called Edmonton House nearby. Both forts were abandoned and rebuilt several times along the North Saskatchewan River. In 1821, the two fur-trading companies merged under the Hudson's Bay Company name. In 1830, the company built Fort Edmonton on the spot where the Alberta Legislature now stands. Fort Edmonton soon became a major trading post.

Over the next fifty years, settlers built homes and businesses around the fort. When gold was discovered in the Klondike in the 1890s, thousands of gold-seekers passed through Edmonton on their way to the north. Some of these people saw the fertile farmland of the Edmonton region and decided to settle there. Edmonton's population steadily increased after 1900, when transcontinental railways opened central Alberta up to European immigration.

Key Events

1795 The North West Company and Hudson's Bay Company establish trading posts in the Edmonton region.

1821 The North West Company merges with the Hudson's Bay Company.

1840 The first Methodist mission in Alberta is established in Edmonton.

The Government

Edmonton became a village in 1871, and an official town in 1892. Soon after becoming a town, Edmonton built a fire hall that also housed the town hall, jail, and police station. By 1904, Edmonton's population had grown to 8,350, and it was proclaimed a city. The Edmonton Charter was the document that detailed Edmonton's incorporation as a city. The charter laid out a new system of government that consisted of a mayor, an appointed commissioner, and a council.

In 1905, the city of Edmonton received another honour. It became the capital city of the newly formed province of Alberta. The Alberta Act of 1905 created Alberta out of a large piece of land called the North-West Territories. Edmonton was chosen as the temporary capital of the province, but several other communities, Calgary in particular, wanted to become the capital city. Over the following months, each community made presentations to the government in a bid to become the official capital. Edmonton remained the favourite choice and was officially declared the capital of Alberta in 1906.

The Alberta provincial government is still based in Edmonton. It sits at the Alberta Legislature. Edmonton's municipal government meets at City Hall, which was built in 1957. A mayor and twelve councillors govern the city.

Edmonton's early government shared a building with the town's constables and its volunteer firefighters.

1869 Canada purchases all of the Hudson's Bay Company's lands, including Fort Edmonton.

1871 Edmonton becomes an official village.

1881 The first newspaper in Alberta, *The Bulletin*, is published.

1891 The Calgary–Edmonton railway opens.

1892 Edmonton is declared a town.

Law and Order

As Alberta's fur trade prospered, trouble and disorder in the area began to grow. Many United States fur-traders arrived in the region to exchange whiskey and other goods for furs. The trading of alcohol, along with dishonest deals and other forms of lawbreaking, brought violence to the region. In 1873, the Canadian government created the North-West Mounted Police (NWMP) to help keep law and order in the western regions. Soon after that, the "A" Troop of the NWMP arrived at Fort Edmonton. This troop maintained the law, and worked to protect the settlers and Native Peoples from unlawful traders.

The town of Edmonton hired its

The first NWMP unit in Fort Edmonton had twenty-two members.

first constable in 1892, less than twenty years after the "A" Troop arrived in the area. As the town developed into a city, Edmonton's police force expanded and evolved. Today, the Edmonton Police Service employs over 1,100 police officers and 300 civilians. It is internationally recognized as a world leader in modern policing.

The town of Edmonton hired its first constable in 1892.

Key Events

1896 Edmonton gains the new role of "Gateway to the North" as the Klondike Gold Rush begins.
1904 Edmonton becomes a city.

1906 Edmonton is named the official capital of Alberta.
1908 The University of Alberta opens.

In 1908, Edmonton had four streetcars running along 21 km of track.

Early Transportation

The railway served as an important connection between communities in the West and larger centres in other parts of Canada and the United States. In 1891, a branch railway opened between Calgary and Strathcona, a community to the southeast of Edmonton. The Canadian Northern Railway reached Edmonton in 1905, and the Grand Trunk Pacific reached the city in 1909.

Royal Canadian Air Force 418 Squadron

During World War II, the city of Edmonton forged a special relationship with one of the **squadrons** of the Royal Canadian Air Force (RCAF). In 1944, the city agreed to "adopt" RCAF 418 Squadron, which was made up of men who were from Edmonton or nearby areas. The men in the squadron had an especially dangerous job: they made regular nighttime flights into enemy territory. After the adoption, the men renamed themselves the "City of Edmonton Squadron." People in Edmonton made special efforts to send treats, such as chewing gum and chocolate, to the men overseas.

The RCAF 418 Squadron destroyed or damaged more enemy aircraft than any other RCAF squadron.

Edmonton's own municipal transportation service was established long before railways made it to the area. In 1908, the Edmonton Radial Railway Service was created, making Edmonton the first city in the Prairies with a public streetcar system. It cost 5 cents to ride on one of four streetcars. In the 1930s, trolley and motor buses were added to the transit system.

1912 Strathcona becomes part of Edmonton.
1947 Petroleum is found at Leduc, near Edmonton.

1978 Edmonton hosts the Commonwealth Games.

Famous People

Alexander Cameron Rutherford 1857–1941

Born in Osgoode, Canada West, Alexander Rutherford set up a successful law practice in South Edmonton in 1895. He was appointed the first premier of Alberta in 1905 and officially elected two months later. Alexander made Edmonton the capital city of the province, chose the site for the Alberta Legislature, and established both the University of Alberta and Alberta Government Telephones. He later helped found the Historical Society of Alberta and was Chancellor of the University of Alberta from 1927 to 1941.

A post-secondary scholarship open to all students in Alberta is named for Alexander Rutherford.

Emily Murphy 1868–1933

Emily Murphy was born in Cookstown, Ontario, and moved to Alberta with her husband in 1905. Two years later the couple moved to Edmonton. In 1910, Emily helped establish the Victoria Order of Nurses in Edmonton. From 1919 to 1921, she was the first president of the Federated Woman's Institute of Canada. In 1916, Emily became the police magistrate of Alberta. She was the first woman to hold this position in the British Empire. She remained magistrate until 1931. Active in many other women's groups, Emily also worked to help get women recognized as "persons" under Canadian law.

Emily Murphy wrote books and articles about Canadian life using the pen name "Janey Canuck."

Mark Messier ranks second in all-time playoff points, goals, and assists.

Mark Messier 1961–

Born and raised in Edmonton, Mark was drafted by the Edmonton Oilers to play in their first season of the NHL in 1979. Mark has won six Stanley cups, five with Edmonton and one with the New York Rangers. Mark was awarded the Conn Smythe Trophy in 1984, and the Hart Trophy in 1990 and 1992. He is ranked fourth in all-time scoring, and has played in more playoff games than any other player in NHL history.

Wayne Gretzky 1961–

Wayne Gretzky started skating on his backyard rink as a toddler in Brantford, Ontario. Even as a child, his talent at hockey was obvious. When he was seventeen and playing in the World Hockey Association (WHA), he was traded to the Edmonton Oilers, who became part of the National Hockey League (NHL) in 1979. In his first year, Wayne tied Marcel Dionne for the most points. Wayne helped the Oilers win the Stanley Cup in 1984, 1985, 1987, and 1988. He also helped Team Canada win the Canada Cup twice. When Wayne was traded to Los Angeles in 1988, many Edmontonians felt as if they had lost their greatest champion. During his career, he won the Hart Trophy for the most valuable player nine times and held many records, including the most career points, most goals, and most assists.

Wayne Gretzky retired from the NHL in 1999.

The Edmonton Grads

The Grads were one of Canada's most famous basketball teams. Formally called the Edmonton Commercial Graduates Basketball Club, this women's basketball team was based at Edmonton's McDougall Commercial High School. The Grads began as a high school team, but grew to rule women's basketball from 1915 to 1940. They won 93 percent of their games, and forty-nine out of fifty-one domestic championship titles. They also won many international championships. During their three European tours, they won all twenty-four games they played. At the time of the team's retirement, they held 108 titles at local, provincial, national, international, and world levels. The Edmonton Grads were considered a national treasure.

Culture

The Arts

Edmonton has a rich variety of visual and performing arts. The Edmonton Art Gallery, which is the oldest public art gallery in the province, was opened in 1924 and exhibits 4,000 Canadian and international paintings, sculptures, photographs, and **performance art** pieces. Artwork is also showcased every summer during The Works: A Visual Arts Celebration.

Each of the five theatres in the Citadel Theatre complex presents impressive and varied performances.

Music lovers can enjoy the Edmonton Opera, one of the top opera companies in Canada. The Edmonton Symphony Orchestra performs concerts of classical music at the Winspear Centre, and the Alberta Conservatory of Music is the second largest conservatory in Canada.

Theatre also thrives in Edmonton. The city has more theatre companies per person than any other city in Canada. The Citadel Theatre complex, with five theatres, is the largest regional theatre building in Canada.

Edmontonians also love to read and write. Many well-known authors live in Edmonton, including Greg Hollingshead and Rudy Weibe, both of whom are winners of the Governor General's Award for Literature.

FESTIVALS

At least fifteen major festivals and events are held in the "City of Festivals" each year. During **Klondike Days** in July, Edmontonians and visitors dress in period costumes to celebrate the importance of the Klondike Gold Rush to the history of Edmonton. Families enjoy the rides and games on the midway, and can try panning for gold.

Summer also brings the **Edmonton Folk Music Festival** and **Jazz City**. Both events feature musicians from around the world.

Annual Celebrations

Edmontonians know how to celebrate the holidays! The city puts great energy into its holiday festivities. The Edmonton Celebrate Canada festival is a ten-day celebration that begins on June 21 with National Aboriginal Day, and ends on July 1, with Canada's birthday. The festival celebrates the country's history and culture, and ends with a great firework demonstration.

From mid-November to December, Hawrelak Park puts on an impressive light display. Edmontonians ring in the New Year with the First Night Festival, a family celebration held downtown. Music, street performers, theatre, and fireworks at midnight are all part of this fun festival.

Along with the rest of Alberta, people in Edmonton also observe Family Day, a holiday to recognize the importance of family. This day is celebrated every year on the third Monday in February. Families in Edmonton and throughout the province can take the day off work or school to spend time together.

Edmonton's First Night Festival is a fun way for families to ring in the New Year together.

The Edmonton International Street Performers Festival is celebrated in July and brings buskers from around the world to perform in Edmonton streets. **The Edmonton Fringe Theatre Festival,** the first of its kind in North America, features more than 1,000 plays and other performances each year and attracts about 450,000 spectators. It is held in August.

Cariwest, the Caribbean Arts Festival, is also celebrated in August. Traditional Caribbean foods, parades, crafts, and music are all a part of the fun.

Ethnic Cuisine

People from many different parts of the world live in Edmonton, and many have brought their distinct cuisines to the city. Citizens and tourists can enjoy just about any type of food imaginable in the city's many local restaurants. Chinese, Indian, Italian, Greek, Korean, Mexican, and Japanese foods are just a few of the ethnic flavours available in the city.

Each year during Klondike Days, the Taste of Edmonton festival allows

Edmonton's trendy Whyte Avenue has many outdoor cafés and patios.

Ukrainian Borscht

- 1.5 litres (6 cups) beef stock
- 1.5 litres (6 cups) water
- 1 medium onion, chopped
- 2 medium beets cut into thin strips
- 1 small carrot, cut into thin strips
- 1 medium potato, diced
- 175 ml (2/3 cup) sliced celery
- 500 ml (2 cups) shredded cabbage
- 1 can white beans
- 250 ml (1 cup) tomato juice
- lemon juice
- salt and pepper
- chopped fresh dill weed
- sour cream

Add the onions and beets to the stock and water. Cook for about 10 minutes. Add the other vegetables. Cook for another 10 minutes. Add the cabbage, and cook until tender. Add the beans and the tomato juice. Season to taste with lemon juice, salt, and pepper, and bring to a boil. Add a handful of dill and ladle into bowls. Before serving, add a spoonful of sour cream into the centre of each bowl.

visitors to taste foods from a variety of different cuisines. Thirty-six restaurants set up **pavilions** offering food. Many Ukrainian dishes can be found at the Taste of Edmonton. A significant number of Edmontonians are of Ukrainian descent. Typical Ukrainian foods include perogies, holubtsi, kielbasa, and borscht.

The Edmonton Mosaic

People from many different ethnic backgrounds call Edmonton home. Immigration has played an important role in the city's growth. Almost half of the city's residents have some British ancestry, but a significant number of residents have German or Ukrainian ancestry. Many people of Chinese descent also live in Edmonton, as well as people of Japanese, Korean, Filipino, Arab, and African descent.

Since 1975, Edmonton has celebrated its many different cultures with the annual Heritage Days Festival. The festival bills itself as the "world's largest three-day celebration of cultural diversity." It has pavilions representing up to sixty different cultures. Visitors to the festival can experience the various cultures by trying ethnic foods and watching traditional performances.

The Ukrainian Cultural Heritage Village

By 1930, about 250,000 Ukrainians had come to Canada. Many settled in or around Edmonton. The Ukrainian Canadian Archives and Museum of Alberta is located in Edmonton. It displays artifacts, papers, and books on Ukrainians in Alberta. The Ukrainian Cultural Heritage Village is situated about 35 km east of Edmonton. This village portrays the pre-1930 lifestyle of the Ukrainian settlers, with demonstrations and over thirty restored buildings, including historic homes, stores, and churches.

The popular Heritage Days Festival takes place in Hawrelak Park over the August long weekend.

People from many different ethnic backgrounds call Edmonton home.

The Economy

Diverse Industries

Edmonton has a diverse economy. The city has long been the transportation and distribution centre for Canada's northern communities, earning it the nickname "Gateway to the North." Edmonton's function as a gateway brought important growth to the city during World War II. It served as a temporary home and materials base for thousands of American troops and construction workers who came to build the Alaska Highway. Edmonton's biggest boom, however, began in February 1947, when oil was discovered at Leduc, about 50 km southwest of the city. This discovery brought thousands of oil-seekers to the area. As more drilling took place, more oil and gas discoveries were made. These discoveries resulted in an enormous **petrochemical** industry. Today, the petrochemical industry

Edmonton is known as the oil capital of Canada. Enough crude oil is processed each day in metro Edmonton to change the oil of every car in Canada.

continues to be a major contributor to Edmonton's economy.

Edmonton has made a successful effort to develop other industries as well. These include meatpacking, food processing, and the manufacturing of plastics and fertilizers. The city is also home to important research centres specializing in technologies, pharmaceuticals, and the oil industry.

As oil prices soared, modern skyscrapers sprung up in Edmonton.

Serving the City

Many Edmontonians work for one of the three levels of government: municipal, provincial, or federal. The provincial government is Edmonton's largest employer. Many government employees who live in the city are elected officials, but others are civil servants who work in certain government departments. Civil servants might be computer programmers, librarians, caretakers, or secretaries.

Edmonton's service sector is very important to the city's economy. Many people in Edmonton work in jobs that are part of this industry, providing

The service industry employs 83 percent of the workers in Edmonton.

various services for others. Health care workers, teachers, salespeople, waiters, and bankers are just some of the people who make up the city's service sector. A large number of Edmontonians work in the tourism industry because the city is a popular destination for tourists and for visiting government officials or businesspeople.

The government of Alberta employs 14,012 Edmontonians, many of whom work in offices at the Alberta Legislature.

Getting Around in Edmonton

It is easy to get around in Edmonton. The Edmonton Transit system has bus routes throughout the city. There are twenty major transit centres where transit users can transfer from one bus to another. As well as regular buses, the city has special low-floor buses and nearly 100 trolley buses.

Edmonton's extensive river valley pathway system is shared by cyclists, joggers, pedestrians, and in-line skaters.

Edmonton was the first North American city with a population of less than 1 million to build and operate an LRT system.

The Light Rail Transit (LRT) is another way for people to get around. It runs 12.8 km from the northeast community of Clareview to the University of Alberta. The LRT system has ten stations, six of which are underground. Like all other major cities, Edmonton has a large number of taxi companies that can take **commuters** from one location to another quickly.

Edmonton also has a number of excellent pathways. Cyclists can travel throughout the city on one of the many multi-use trails or bike routes. Downtown, pedestrians can walk through the many covered walkways, called pedways, that connect buildings.

Electrical Buses

Trolley buses were first introduced in Edmonton in 1939 as a replacement for streetcars, which were wearing down the roadways. The city purchased six trolleys built by British companies, and became the third city in Canada to have trolley buses. These buses are powered by electricity from overhead wires. Edmonton has 127 km of trolley bus routes.

Smart City

Edmonton has been called a "smart city" because of its excellent educational institutions and its focus on research. Edmonton is home to the University of Alberta, which is the largest university in the province. It has about 30,000 full-time students. The largest college in the province, Grant MacEwan College, is also located in Edmonton, as is Athabasca University, one of the largest distance-learning universities in the world. The Northern Alberta Institute of Technology (NAIT) is another respected educational institution based in the city. About four out of every ten working people in Edmonton have post-secondary degrees or diplomas. Edmonton also has the highest number of post-secondary graduates per capita in Canada.

Edmonton is a major centre for research and technology. The city has many advanced technology companies. At the Edmonton Research Park, more than thirty public and private organizations, and over 1,200 employees, carry out research in areas such as medicine, computer software, and electronics.

The University of Alberta campus covers about fifty city blocks and has over ninety buildings. There is also an off-campus research facility.

Sports and Recreation

Green Space

Edmonton has a great deal of green space. In fact, the Edmonton river valley is considered to be one of the largest stretches of urban parkland in North America. It is made up of twenty-two parks, four lake systems, and 150 km of trails. Cyclists, runners, in-line skaters, and walkers use the river valley's system of pathways and trails. In the winter, many people cross-country ski

Elk Island National Park is less than an hour away from Edmonton. The park is a wilderness protection area.

or snowshoe along the trails. More than two million people make use of these trails every year.

Edmonton also has a number of city parks, playgrounds, and open areas to enjoy throughout the seasons. There are over fifty public golf courses in the greater Edmonton area, as well as two National Parks—Jasper and Elk Island—and nine provincial parks within close driving distance to and from the city.

There are a number of excellent indoor sporting facilities in Edmonton.

Edmonton's pathways are used and enjoyed year-round.

The Commonwealth Stadium Recreation Centre, the Kinsmen Sports Centre, and Mill Woods Recreation Centre offer indoor activities such as swimming, diving, racquetball, and squash.

City of Champions

Edmonton's sports teams have a history of winning. The Edmonton Eskimos are a part of the Canadian Football League. They play in the Commonwealth Stadium, and have won the Grey Cup five times in a row, from 1978 to 1982.

The Edmonton Oilers are a team in the National Hockey League. They have won five Stanley Cups: in 1984, 1985, 1987, 1988 and 1990. The Edmonton Trappers baseball team became the first Canadian team to win the Pacific Coast League Championship in 1984. The Trappers, who were named "Team of the Year" by Baseball America Magazine in 1996, won the championships again in 1996 and 1997. Edmonton is also home to the Edmonton Drillers of the National Professional Soccer League.

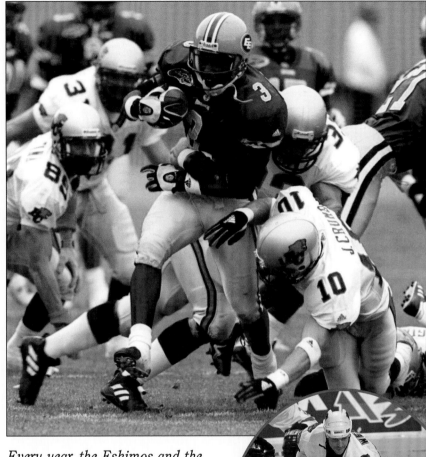

Every year, the Eskimos and the Calgary Stampeders battle it out in the annual Labour Day classic.

The Oilers play all of their home games at the Skyreach Centre, which holds 16,000 fans.

Cowboy Competition

During the Canadian Finals Rodeo, held in November, the best professional rodeo riders in the country gather in Edmonton to compete. The events include calf roping, steer wrestling, and saddle bronc and bull riding. The rodeo has some of the largest cash prizes of any rodeo in Canada.

Tourism

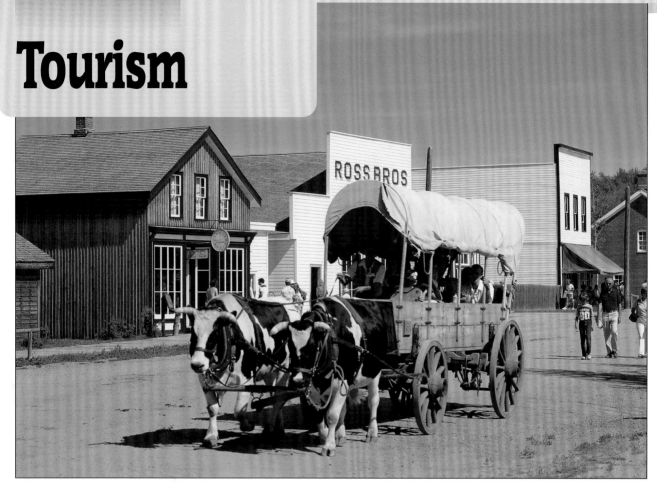

A Trip to the Past

Fort Edmonton Park is a popular destination for visitors to Edmonton. The park is a living-history museum, depicting Edmonton during four stages of its history—a fur-trading fort in 1846, a frontier town in 1885, a developing capital in 1905, and a blossoming business community in 1920.

Among the exhibits at Fort Edmonton Park is a reconstruction of the old Fort Edmonton fur-trading post; a 1885 street, complete with a blacksmith shop, saloon, and general store; a 1905 street with an old fire hall and fire engines; and a 1920 street with a **confectionary** shop and a functioning streetcar. Employees dressed in period

Wagon tours are a fun, leisurely way to see Fort Edmonton Park.

costumes give demonstrations and encourage visitors to participate in period activities such as playing horseshoes or driving antique cars.

Visitors to the park can ride the streetcars or the historic steam train.

A Shopper's Delight

West Edmonton Mall is one of Alberta's biggest tourist attractions. This enormous mall has over 800 stores, and more than 110 restaurants. It is

West Edmonton Mall is the only mall of its kind in Canada. It is both a shopper's paradise and a major entertainment centre.

West Edmonton Mall's trained dolphins perform daily for visitors.

also home to twenty-six movie theatres, the Fantasyland Hotel, an aquarium, and an indoor ice rink.

One of West Edmonton Mall's most popular features is its amusement park. Galaxyland is considered the largest indoor amusement park in the world. It offers twenty-five rides and attractions, including a triple-loop roller coaster and a 13-storey free-fall ride. The mall also features the Deep Sea Adventure, where visitors can take a submarine ride or watch a live dolphin show. At the World Waterpark, visitors can enjoy many different water slides, swim in one of the world's largest wave pools, or relax on an indoor beach. Visitors will have a hard time running out of things to do at West Edmonton Mall.

The Space and Science Centre

Housing the largest planetarium dome in Canada, the Edmonton Space and Science Centre has an IMAX theatre, computer labs, and various science exhibits. The Challenger Learning Centre allows visitors to experience what it would be like to go on a space mission. The Margaret Zeidler Theatre puts on music laser light shows with the aid of projectors controlled by computers. In the public **observatory**, visitors can take a good look at the moon, the stars, and the planets.

Alberta's Museum

The Provincial Museum of Alberta is one of the most popular museums in Canada. The museum opened during Canada's **centennial** in 1967. It is home to one of the largest collections of Hudson's Bay Company fur-trade memorabilia. It also displays the largest assortment of mounted birds in Canada.

The museum exhibits seven collections of natural history artifacts from Alberta, including **botanical**, geological, and animal artifacts. Social history is represented in exhibits that depict such subjects as the First Nations peoples of Alberta, early

In the Bug Room, visitors can view insects, both dead and alive.

government history, and recent western Canadian history.

In the Bug Room, visitors can view insects, both dead and alive. One cabinet contains specimens of pinned Alberta insects, and serves as an aid to visitors who wish to identify insects they have seen. Live leafcutter ants, scorpions, and walking sticks housed in enclosures similar to their natural habitats allow visitors to learn more about how insects live.

The Provincial Museum of Alberta is committed to representing Alberta's Native Peoples.

Visitors to the Bug Room can play with a stick insect and see the largest tarantula species on Earth.

Muttart Conservatory

The Muttart Conservatory is a must-see for plant-lovers. The conservatory is made up of five glass houses, shaped like pyramids, that house all kinds of plants and flowers. Three of the pyramids have a theme and support plants from different climatic zones. The Arid Pavilion has a desert climate and displays flowering cacti. The Tropical Pavilion has a waterfall and plants from the tropics. The Temperate Pavilion shows many different plants from North America. Another pyramid at the conservatory is used to house changing displays throughout the year. The fifth pyramid is smaller than the rest, and features an impressive mural.

Tourists have been visiting the Muttart pyramids since they were officially opened in September 1976.

The History of Alberta Flight

The Alberta Aviation Museum contains exhibits of the province's rich aviation history. The first airplanes flew in Alberta in 1909. Bush pilots in the 1920s and 1930s made regular flights between Edmonton, the Canadian North, and Alaska. The Aviation Museum displays several planes, including a "Mosquito" from World War II.

Architecture

A Home for the Provincial Government

When Alberta became a province in 1905, the provincial government did not yet have a building in which to meet. The opening ceremonies and swearing-in of the province's first Legislative Assembly were held at the Thistle Roller and Ice Rink. The assembly conducted government business at a nearby school. After officially deciding that Edmonton would be Alberta's capital city, the government chose the location of the future Alberta Legislature—the North Saskatchewan River bank.

Allan Merrick Jeffers, the provincial architect of Alberta, designed the Alberta Legislature. His design included a T-shaped floor plan, huge columns in the entrance, and a large dome.

The materials used to build the Alberta Legislature came from all over the world. The outside first-storey walls are made from granite from Vancouver Island. The remaining storeys are made from sandstone from the Calgary area. The columns and walls of the **rotunda** are made from green marble from Pennsylvania, while the darker green marble in the Chamber came from Belgium. The floors and staircases are made from grey marble from Quebec, while a darker grey marble from Italy was used at the base of the columns and walls.

Construction of the Alberta Legislature began in 1907 and was completed in 1912.

The park that surrounds the Alberta Legislature was created in the 1970s for Albertans and tourists to enjoy.

Restoring Older Structures

Edmonton has restored many of its beautiful old structures. Government House was completed in 1913. From then until 1938, the mansion was the home of Alberta's Lieutenant Governor. The building then served as a World War II veteran's hospital from 1944 to 1950. For many years after that, it was a home for disabled veterans. Government House was restored and reopened as the Alberta government conference centre in 1976.

One of Edmonton's most spectacular buildings is the Hotel Macdonald, which sits high up on the bank of the North Saskatchewan River. Canadian Pacific opened the hotel in 1915. The hotel underwent a $28 million makeover and was reopened in 1991. Today the hotel has 198 rooms.

Hotel Macdonald stands majestically as Edmonton's historic downtown landmark.

The Al Rashid Mosque

During the 1930s, Muslims in Edmonton decided to build a **mosque** in their community. To fund the construction, they asked for help from Muslims around Alberta and elsewhere in Canada. The Al Rashid Mosque was completed in 1938, making it the oldest mosque in North America. Prayers, weddings, and funerals were held on the first floor of the mosque, while social events and business meetings were held in the basement of the building. In 1946, the mosque was moved to a new location a few blocks from where it was originally built. In 1990, the Al Rashid Mosque moved to Fort Edmonton Park.

Fascinating Facts

1 To commemorate Alberta's 75th anniversary, the city of Edmonton installed an artificial waterfall on the High Level Bridge. The waterfall is 7.3 m higher than Niagara Falls. It runs on Sunday evenings and Saturday afternoons during Klondike Days. The Great Divide Waterfall is 90 m wide and 63 m high.

2 Edmonton was awarded the Communities in Bloom award for most beautiful city in Canada with a population over 300,000 in 1997, 1998, and 2000.

3 Edmonton has more green space than any other city in Canada.

4 Victoria Golf Course, which was purchased in 1910 by the city, is the oldest municipal golf course in Canada.

5 Edmonton's municipal airport was the first municipal airport in Canada. It was opened in 1927.

6 According to the Guinness Book of World Records, West Edmonton Mall is the largest shopping centre in the world. The mall's parking lot is also the largest in the world.

7 Edmonton was struck by a devastating tornado on July 31, 1987. Twenty-seven people were killed.

8 Edmonton is the sunniest city in Canada, receiving more than 2,263 hours of sunshine on average each year.

9 The five large trees that sit in pots in the gallery of the Alberta Legislature have grown from palm seeds given to Alberta by the government of California in 1932.

10 Actor Michael J. Fox, writer W.P. Kinsella, and educator and theorist Marshall McLuhan were all born in Edmonton.

Activities

Based on what you have read, try to answer the following questions.

Multiple Choice:

1 Which of the following authors is not from Edmonton?
a) W.P Kinsella
b) W.O. Mitchell
c) Rudy Wiebe
d) Greg Hollingshead

2 Edmonton gets:
a) More sunshine than any other Canadian city.
b) More snow than any other major Canadian city.
c) Less sun than any other major Canadian city.
d) More tornadoes than any other major Canadian city.

3 Which of the following foods is not typically Ukrainian?
a) perogies
b) cabbage rolls
c) hummus
d) borscht

4 The Guinness Book of World Records considers West Edmonton Mall to be the largest shopping centre in the world. What other record does the mall hold?
a) Largest waterpark
b) Largest number of dolphins held in captivity
c) Most restaurants under one roof
d) Largest parking lot in the world

5 What was the name of the fort that was built around the same time as the original Fort Edmonton?
a) Fort Hawrelak
b) Fort Strathcona
c) Fort Jasper
d) Fort Augustus

True or False:

6 Wayne Gretzky was born in Edmonton.

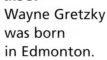

7 Edmonton has often been referred to as Gateway to the West.

8 The Citadel Theatre complex is the largest of its kind in Canada.

9 Edmonton was named capital of Alberta in 1904.

10 Edmonton is considered the sunniest city in Canada.

1. b; 2. a; 3. c; 4. d; 5. d; 6. False. He was born in Brantford, Ontario. 7. False. It has been referred to as "Gateway to the North." 8. True. 9. False. Edmonton was named the official capital of Alberta in 1906. 10. True.

More Information

Books

Arminas, David. **Edmonton, The Untold Story**. Montgomery, Alabama: Community Communications, 1998.

Beckett, Harry. **Eye on Canada: Alberta**. Calgary: Weigl Educational Publishers, 2001.

Christensen, Jo-Anne and Dennis Shapka. **An Edmonton Album**. Toronto: Hounslow Press, 1999.

Schemenauer, Elma. **Hello Edmonton**. Agincourt: GLC Silver Burdett, 1986.

Web sites

The City of Edmonton Web site

http://www.gov.edmonton.ab.ca/

Edmonton, a Smart City

http://www.smartcity.edmonton.ab.ca/

See-Edmonton Online Guide

http://www.see-edmonton.com/

Edmonton Oilers

http://www.edmontonoilers.com

Edmonton Eskimos

http://www.esks.com

Muttart Conservatory

http://www.gov.edmonton.ab.ca/muttart/

Some Web sites stay current longer than others. To find information on Edmonton, use your Internet search engine to look up such topics as "West Edmonton Mall," "Fort Edmonton," "Klondike Days," or any other topic you want to research.

Glossary

botanical: referring to plants

centennial: a hundredth birthday

commuters: people who must travel from one point to another

confectionary: a place where sweets are made and sold

Klondike: the region in the Yukon Territory where gold was discovered in 1896

mosque: a place where Muslims go to worship

observatory: a building or room that is equipped with telescopes and designed for looking into space

pavilions: structures, often tents, used at fairs and in parks

performance art: a type of performance that often fuses different art forms, such as music, dance, or drama, together

petrochemical: an oil and gas product

rotunda: a large circular room with a dome

squadrons: groups of armed troops

Index

Alberta Aviation Museum 25

Alberta Legislature 6, 7, 10, 17, 26, 29

Calgary 7, 9, 21, 26

Cree 6

Edmonton Grads 11

Edmonton Space and Science Centre 23

Fort Edmonton 6, 7, 8, 22, 30, 31

Fort Edmonton Park 22, 27

Government House 27

Gretzky, Wayne 11, 30

Heritage Days 5, 15

Hotel Macdonald 27

Hudson's Bay Company 6, 7, 24

Klondike Days 5, 12, 14, 28, 31

manufacturing 16

Messier, Mark 11

Murphy, Emily 10

Muttart Conservatory 25, 31

North West Company 6

oil 16

Provincial Museum of Alberta 24

railways 6, 7, 9

Rutherford, Alexander Cameron 10

sports teams 21, 31

Strathcona 9, 30

West Edmonton Mall 23, 29, 30, 31